NATURAL DISASTERS
Blizzards

by Betsy Rathburn

BLASTOFF! READERS

3

BELLWETHER MEDIA • MINNEAPOLIS, MN

Note to Librarians, Teachers, and Parents:

Blastoff! Readers are carefully developed by literacy experts and combine standards-based content with developmentally appropriate text.

Level 1 provides the most support through repetition of high-frequency words, light text, predictable sentence patterns, and strong visual support.

Level 2 offers early readers a bit more challenge through varied simple sentences, increased text load, and less repetition of high-frequency words.

Level 3 advances early-fluent readers toward fluency through increased text and concept load, less reliance on visuals, longer sentences, and more literary language.

Level 4 builds reading stamina by providing more text per page, increased use of punctuation, greater variation in sentence patterns, and increasingly challenging vocabulary.

Level 5 encourages children to move from "learning to read" to "reading to learn" by providing even more text, varied writing styles, and less familiar topics.

Whichever book is right for your reader, Blastoff! Readers are the perfect books to build confidence and encourage a love of reading that will last a lifetime!

This edition first published in 2020 by Bellwether Media, Inc.

No part of this publication may be reproduced in whole or in part without written permission of the publisher. For information regarding permission, write to Bellwether Media, Inc., Attention: Permissions Department, 6012 Blue Circle Drive, Minnetonka, MN 55343.

Library of Congress Cataloging-in-Publication Data

Names: Rathburn, Betsy, author.
Title: Blizzards / by Betsy Rathburn.
Description: Minneapolis, MN : Bellwether Media, Inc., 2020. | Series:
   Blastoff! Readers. Natural Disasters | Audience: Ages 5-8. | Audience: K
   to grade 3. | Includes bibliographical references and index.
Identifiers: LCCN 2019001508 (print) | LCCN 2019003087 (ebook) | ISBN
   9781618915658 (ebook) | ISBN 9781644870242 (hardcover : alk. paper) | ISBN
   9781618917454 (pbk. : alk. paper)
Subjects: LCSH: Blizzards--Juvenile literature. | Winter storms--Juvenile literature.
Classification: LCC QC926.37 (ebook) | LCC QC926.37 R3765 2020 (print) | DDC 551.55/5--dc23
LC record available at https://lccn.loc.gov/2019001508

Editor: Al Albertson   Designer: Josh Brink

Printed in the United States of America, North Mankato, MN

Table of Contents

What Are Blizzards?

Blizzards are strong winter storms. They usually hit flat **plains** and high mountaintops. In the United States, they are common in **Blizzard Alley**.

These cold storms bring howling wind and blowing snow. This sometimes leads to disaster!

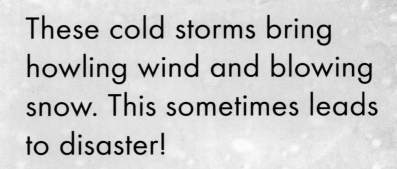

Blizzard Alley

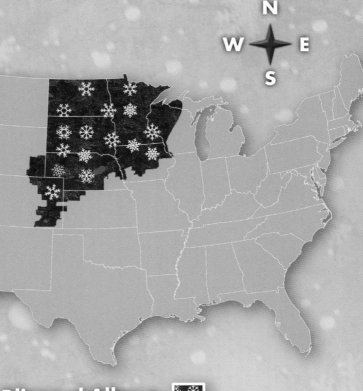

Blizzard Alley =

Blizzards form when warm, wet winds meet cold, dry winds. The warm air moves upward. The cold winds rush in below.

Clouds form when the rising air holds a lot of **moisture**. If winds are cold enough, the moisture falls as snow!

How Blizzards Form

warm air —

cold air

Strong winds blow the falling snow. Blizzards bring wind speeds of 35 miles (56 kilometers) per hour or more.

Blizzards last for at least three hours. **Visibility** is limited to 0.25 miles (0.4 kilometers) or less!

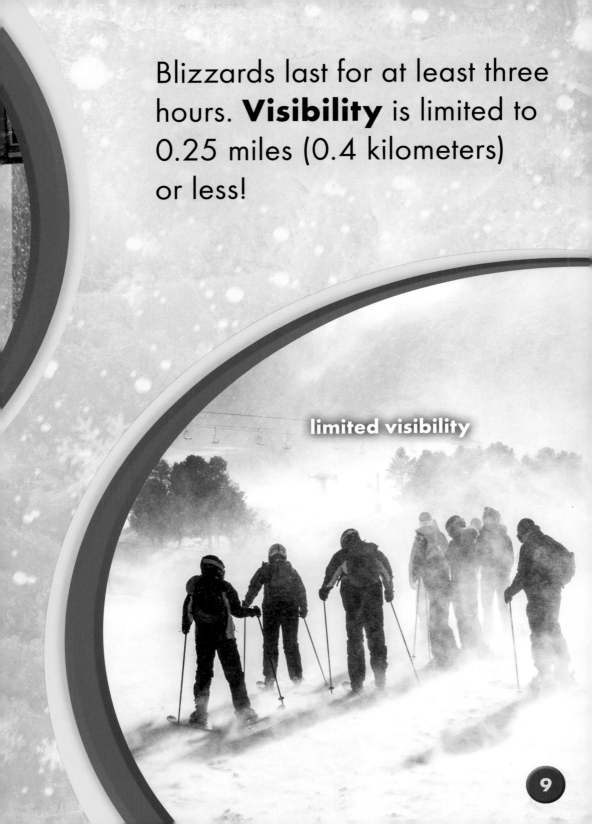

limited visibility

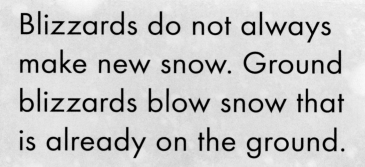

Blizzards do not always make new snow. Ground blizzards blow snow that is already on the ground.

Ground blizzards can be just as dangerous as other blizzards!

ground blizzard

Blizzard Damage

whiteout

Blizzards cause big problems. Blowing snow brings **whiteouts**. These make it hard to travel to school or work.

12

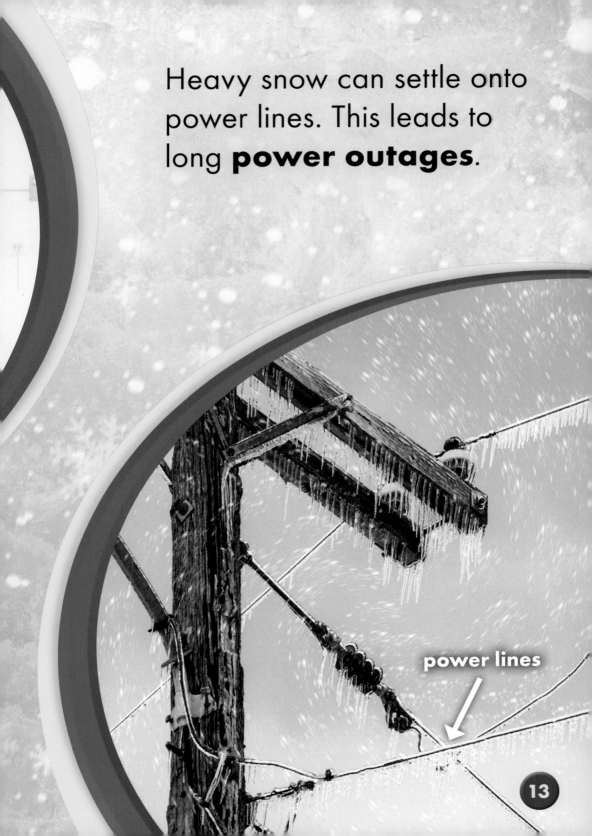

Heavy snow can settle onto power lines. This leads to long **power outages**.

power lines

Low **windchill** can lead to **frostbite**. People stuck outside are in danger.

Some people do not have warm shelter. Others must leave home for work. These people are most at risk during blizzards.

Windchill Danger

Temperature (°F/°C)

Wind Speed (miles per hour/ kilometers per hour)	30/-1	10/-12	0/-18	-10/-23	-20/-29	-30/-34	-40/-40
0/0	30/-1	10/-12	0/-18	-10/-23	-20/-29	-30/-34	-40/-40
5/8	25/-4	1/-17	-11/-24	-22/-30	-34/-37	-46/-43	-57/-49
10/16	21/-6	-4/-20	-16/-27	-28/-33	-41/-41	-53/-47	-66-54
15/24	-19/-7	-7/-22	-13/-25	-32/-36	-45/-43	-58/-50	-71/-57
20/32	-17/-8	-9/-23	-15/-26	-35/-37	-48/-44	-61/-52	-74/-59
25/40	-16/-9	-11/-24	-17/-27	-37/-38	-51/-46	-64/-53	-78/-61
30/48	- 15/-9	- 12/-24	-19/-28	- 39/-39	- 53/-47	- 71/-57	-80/-62

☐ = little danger of frostbite
☐ = danger of frostbite
☐ = frostbite in one minute
☐ = frostbite in 30 seconds

Predicting Disaster

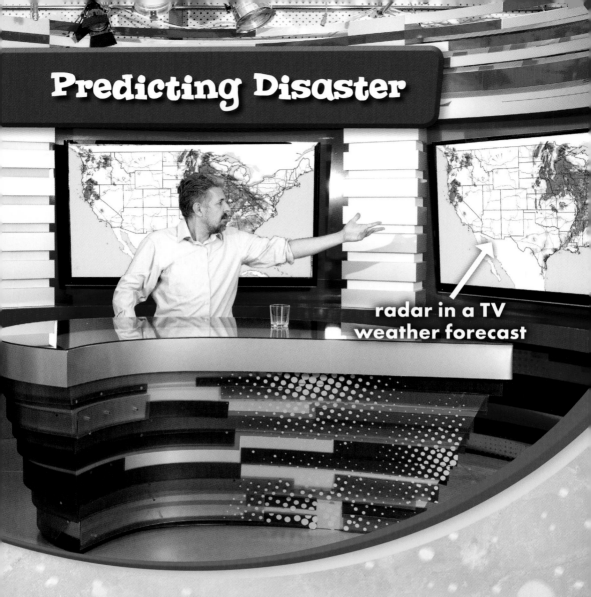

radar in a TV weather forecast

Meteorologists can **forecast** blizzards. **Satellites** help meteorologists see Earth from above. **Radar** helps them spot changes in the **atmosphere**.

Meteorologists send out warnings when blizzards begin to form!

HEAVY SNOW ROADS MAY BE CLOSED

There are other blizzard warning signs, too. Strong winds may bring cold weather. They may also cause **snowdrifts**.

These clues could mean a blizzard is coming. Time to find shelter!

snowdrift

Blizzard Profile

Name: February 2010 North American blizzard

Dates: February 5-6, 2010

Location: northeastern United States, California, New Mexico, and Mexico

Damage to Property:
- power lines downed by heavy snow
- several buildings caved in
- cars left on blocked roads for days

Damage to People:
- at least 30 lives lost
- thousands of people left without power

February 2010
North American blizzard

It is best to stay inside when blizzards are in the forecast. Roads may be dangerous. It is easy to get lost.

People must prepare for blizzards. These dangerous natural disasters cannot be stopped!

preparing for a blizzard

Glossary

atmosphere—the air surrounding Earth

Blizzard Alley—a region of the northern United States where blizzards are most likely to occur

forecast—to make a guess about future weather events based on collected information

frostbite—an injury that occurs when the skin is exposed to cold for too long

meteorologists—scientists who study weather

moisture—water or other liquid

plains—areas of flat, open land

power outages—events in which no electricity is available

radar—a system that measures direction, distance, and speed; radar can track storms.

satellites—machines that circle Earth to collect information

snowdrifts—large hills of snow created when wind blows snow

visibility—the distance a person is able to see

whiteouts—events in which blowing snow makes it impossible to see

windchill—a measurement of how cold the air feels based on temperature and wind speed

To Learn More

AT THE LIBRARY
Bowman, Chris. *Survive a Blizzard*. Minneapolis, Minn.: Bellwether Media, 2017.

Johnson, Robin. *What Is A Blizzard?* New York, N.Y.: Crabtree Publishing Company, 2016.

Murray, Julie. *Blizzards*. Minneapolis, Minn.: Abdo Zoom, 2018.

ON THE WEB

FACTSURFER

Factsurfer.com gives you a safe, fun way to find more information.

1. Go to www.factsurfer.com.

2. Enter "blizzards" into the search box and click 🔍.

3. Select your book cover to see a list of related web sites.

Index

The images in this book are reproduced through the courtesy of: Art Konovalov, cover (hero); Bronwyn Photo, cover (snow); Lucky Business, cover (background); Andrew Mayovskyy, CIP (background); Supertrooper, CIP (snow); ronya, p. 4; onebluelight, p. 6; Nathaniel Noir/ Alamy, p. 8; Webkatrin001, p. 9; cmannphoto, p. 10; CribbVisuals, p. 11; Alex Erwin, p. 12; ArtBitz, p. 13; tommaso79, p. 14; Andrey Burmakin, p. 16; Alan Budman, p. 17; timsa, p. 18; The Washington Post/ Getty Images, p. 19; Yugano Konstantin, p. 20; Carolyn Kaster/ AP Images, p. 21.